Not Your Fault

50 Inspirations for Teenagers of Divorcing Parents

Terry Winner

"Not Your Fault" cover design by Terry Winner

Introduction

Divorce can be a difficult and stressful time for teenagers, but it doesn't have to be.

This book of inspirational quotes and phrases is designed to provide support and guidance to teens who are experiencing their parents' divorce. It contains powerful words of encouragement and advice to help teens find strength and hope during this difficult time.

The phrases and their expanded explanations in this book are designed to give teenagers the tools to cope with the emotions and challenges of their parents' divorce, and to move forward in a positive and healthy way.

It's important for parents to be aware of the impact that divorce can have on their children, and to take steps to ensure that their children are supported and their needs are met during this difficult time.

It is essential to remember that teenagers are still developing and need support and understanding during this time. Talk to them openly and honestly about the divorce and to answer any questions they may have. Provide them with emotional support and to let them know that they can talk to you about their feelings.

Be aware of the potential changes that may come with divorce. This could include changes in living arrangements, changes in school, or changes in family dynamics. It's important to be aware of these changes and to be prepared to help your child adjust to them.

There can sometimes be the potential for conflict between divorcing parents. It's important to try to keep the conflict between the parents away from the children, and to try to keep the children out of the middle of any disputes.

Remember that divorce can be a difficult and stressful time for teenage children, but it doesn't have to be. With the right support and understanding, teenagers can get through this difficult time and come out stronger on the other side.

Terry Winner

1. "It's OK to feel overwhelmed, but don't forget you are resilient and capable of overcoming anything."

We all need help from time to time, and it's important to remember that asking for help doesn't make you weak.

In fact, it can be a sign of strength and resilience. It takes courage to admit that you need help, and it's a sign of maturity to recognize when you need assistance.

When you're feeling overwhelmed or struggling with a problem, it's important to reach out for help. Whether it's a friend, family member, or professional, don't be afraid to ask for help.

It's OK to not have all the answers, and it's OK to need a little extra support.

When you're asking for help, it's important to be honest and open about your needs. Explain what you're going through and why you need help. Be specific about what kind of help you need, and be sure to express your appreciation for any assistance you receive.

It's also important to remember that you don't have to go it alone. There are many resources available to help you, such as hotlines, online support groups, and mental health professionals.

Don't be afraid to take advantage of these resources if you need them.

2. "You are not alone in your struggles and you will get through this."

It can be hard to cope with the struggles life throws at us. We all experience difficult times, and it can be overwhelming to try and make sense of it all. But it's important to remember that you are not alone in your struggles. There are people out there who understand and are willing to help.

When you're feeling overwhelmed, it's important to take a step back and take a break. Take some time to do something that makes you feel good, like listening to music, going for a walk, or talking to a friend. This can help to clear your head and give you some perspective.

It's also important to reach out for help when you need it. Talk to a trusted friend or family member, or seek professional help if necessary. There are many resources available to help you cope with your struggles, including counselling, support groups, and online resources.

Remember that you will get through this. It may take time, but with the right support and resources, you can find a way to cope with your struggles and move forward.

Don't be afraid to ask for help and take the time to take care of yourself. You are strong and capable, and you will get through this.

3. "The way you feel today is not the way you will feel tomorrow."

We all have days when we feel down, overwhelmed, or just plain exhausted. It can be hard to remember that these feelings are only temporary and that tomorrow can bring a new perspective.

It's important to remember that the way you feel today is not the way you will feel tomorrow.

No matter how bad things seem today, it's important to remember that tomorrow is a new day and a new opportunity to start fresh. It's important to take a step back and remember that the current situation is only temporary.

It's easy to get stuck in a negative mindset, but it's important to remember that things can and will get better.

It's important to take care of yourself and to practice self-care. Take some time to do something that makes you feel good.

Whether it's reading a book, going for a walk, or spending time with friends, it's important to take a break and focus on yourself. Doing something that brings you joy can help to shift your mindset and give you the motivation to keep going.

It's also important to remember that you are not alone. Reach out to friends and family for support. Talking to someone can help to put things into perspective and can help to remind you that you are not alone.

The way you feel today is not the way you will feel tomorrow. It's easy to get stuck in a negative mindset, but it's important to know that things can and will get better.

Take some time to take care of yourself and to practice self-care. Reach out to friends and family for support. Remember that tomorrow is a new day and a new opportunity to start fresh.

4. "Your parents' divorce is not your fault, you are not to blame."

Divorce can be a difficult and emotional experience for everyone involved, especially children. It can be hard to understand why your parents are separating, and it can be easy to blame yourself for the situation. It's important to remember that the decision to divorce is not your fault.

Divorce is a complex issue, and it's often the result of a combination of factors. It's important to remember that the decision to divorce is not something that you can control. It's a decision that your parents have made, and it's not something that you can change.

It's also important to remember that divorce doesn't have to be a negative experience. It can be an opportunity for growth and healing for everyone involved. It's important to talk to your parents about how you're feeling and to let them know that you're there for them.

It's also important to take care of yourself during this time. Make sure you're getting enough sleep, eating healthy, and spending time with friends and family. It's also important to talk to a trusted adult or counsellor if you're feeling overwhelmed or confused.

At the end of the day, it's important to remember that your parents' divorce is not your fault. You are not to blame, and it's important to take care of yourself during this difficult time.

5. *"You are strong enough to face any challenge in life."*

Life is full of challenges, and it can be difficult to face them head on. But it is important to remember that you are strong enough to take on whatever comes your way.

No matter how hard the challenge may seem, you have the strength and resilience to make it through.

When you are faced with a challenge, it is important to take a step back and assess the situation. Take a deep breath and remind yourself that you can handle whatever comes your way.

Think about what resources you have available to you and how you can use them to your advantage.

Once you have taken the time to assess the situation, it is important to take action. Make a plan of action and stick to it.

Break down the challenge into smaller, more manageable tasks and focus on completing them one at a time. This will help you stay focused and motivated.

It is also important to remember to take care of yourself. Make sure you are getting enough rest, eating healthy, and taking time for yourself. Self-care is essential in helping you stay strong and resilient in the face of any challenge.

Always, remember that you are not alone. Reach out to friends and family for support and advice. They can provide a listening ear and help you stay positive and motivated.

No matter what challenge you are facing, remember that you are strong enough to take it on. With the right mindset and support, you can overcome any obstacle.

6. "Your parents still love you, even if they don't love each other."

It's a difficult thing to accept, but it's true: your parents may not love each other any more, but they still love you.

It can be hard to understand why your parents can't get along, and it can be even harder to accept that they may not love each other any more. But it's important to remember that your parents' love for you is still there, even if their love for each other isn't.

Your parents may have gone through a difficult time in their relationship, but that doesn't mean that their love for you has gone away. Even if your parents are no longer together, they still care about you and want the best for you. They may not be able to show it in the same way they used to, but that doesn't mean that their love isn't there.

It's also important to remember that your parents' love for each other doesn't have to define your relationship with them. You can still have a strong relationship with each of your parents, even if they don't love each other any more. You can still talk to them, spend time with them, and rely on them for support.

It's OK to feel sad or confused about your parents' relationship, but it's important to remember that their love for you is still there. Your parents may not love each other any more, but they still love you.

7. "Your feelings are valid and you deserve to express them."

We all experience a wide range of emotions throughout our lives, and it's important to recognize and accept those feelings. Too often, we try to suppress our emotions or ignore them altogether. This can lead to feelings of frustration, resentment, and even depression.

When we validate our feelings, we are acknowledging that they are real and valid. We are recognizing that our emotions are a normal part of life and that it's OK to feel them. This can help us to process our emotions in a healthy way and move forward in a positive direction.

When we don't validate our feelings, we can become overwhelmed and struggle to cope. This can happen when we're feeling overwhelmed or confused.

By taking the time to acknowledge our feelings, we can gain insight into our emotional state and better understand our needs.

Validation can also help us to connect with others. When we are open and honest about our feelings, it can help us to build stronger relationships with those around us. We can learn to empathize with others and understand their perspectives better.

Validating our feelings can help us to take action. When we recognize our emotions, we can make decisions that are based on our true feelings rather than trying to ignore them. This can help us to make positive changes in our lives and take steps towards achieving our goals.

Overall, validating our feelings is an important part of self-care and can help us to lead healthier, happier lives. So the next time you're feeling overwhelmed or frustrated, take a moment to recognize and accept your emotions.

You deserve to be heard and understood.

8. "Remember that you are still the same person you were before the divorce."

Divorce can be a difficult and emotionally draining experience. It can be hard to adjust to the changes that come with it, and it can be difficult to remember that you are still the same person you were before the divorce.

It can be easy to get caught up in the emotions and the stress of the situation, and it can be hard to remember that you are still the same person you were before the divorce.

Be aware that you are still the same person you were before the divorce. You may have changed in some ways, but the core of who you are remains the same.

You may have different goals and priorities now, but you are still the same person. You may have different relationships now, but you are still the same person. You may have different interests now, but you are still the same person.

It is also important to remember that you are not alone. There are many people who have gone through a divorce, and many who are going through it now.

It can be helpful to reach out to these people for support and advice. There are also many resources available to help you through this difficult time.

Always be sure to take care of yourself. Make sure you are getting enough rest, eating healthy, and exercising.

Take time to do things that make you happy, such as spending time with friends and family, reading a book, or taking a walk. Taking care of yourself will help you to stay strong and positive during this difficult time.

9. "You are capable of creating your own happiness and joy."

Creating your own happiness and joy is something that we all strive for in life. It can be difficult to do, especially when life throws us curveballs and we find ourselves in difficult situations. But, it is possible to create your own happiness and joy, no matter what life throws at you.

The first step to creating your own happiness and joy is to recognize that it is within your power to do so. You have the power to choose how you respond to any situation and to create a positive outlook for yourself.

Remember that you are in control of your own happiness and joy, and that you can choose to make the best of any situation.

The next step is to focus on the things that bring you joy and happiness. This could be anything from spending time with friends and family, to engaging in activities that you enjoy.

It is important to take time for yourself and to focus on the things that bring you joy and happiness.

Take some time to practice self-care and to take care of your mental and physical health.

Taking care of yourself is essential for creating your own happiness and joy. This could include getting enough sleep, eating healthy, exercising, and taking time to relax and unwind.

Finally, it is important to practice gratitude and to appreciate the good things in life. Taking time to be thankful for the good things in life can help to create a positive outlook and to bring more joy and happiness into your life.

10. "It's OK to take your time to process what's happening and to find your own path."

Navigating life can be a difficult journey, especially when faced with difficult decisions and unexpected changes. It can be hard to know what to do and how to move forward.

However, it's OK to take your time to process what's happening and to find your own path.

When faced with a difficult decision, it can be helpful to take a step back and look at the situation from a different perspective. Ask yourself questions like:

- What are the pros and cons of each option?
- What are the potential outcomes?
- What are the risks?
- What are the benefits?

Taking the time to consider all of these factors can help you make an informed decision.

It can also be helpful to talk to people you trust and respect. Talking to someone who has been through a similar situation can provide valuable insight and help you gain a better understanding of the situation.

It can also be helpful to talk to a professional who can provide unbiased advice and help you make the best decision for you.

It's important to remember that there is no right or wrong answer when it comes to making decisions. Everyone's situation is different and what works for one person may not work for another.

It's OK to take your time to process what's happening and to find your own path.

At the end of the day, it's important to trust yourself and your instincts. You know yourself better than anyone else and you are the only one who can make the best decision for you.

Take the time to consider all of the options and trust that you will make the right decision.

11. "It's OK to ask for help — it doesn't make you weak."

We all need help from time to time. Whether it's a problem at work, a personal issue, or a difficult decision, it's good to know that asking for help doesn't make you weak. In fact, it takes strength and courage to reach out and ask for assistance.

When we're struggling with something, it can be hard to admit that we need help. We may feel embarrassed or ashamed, or worry that we'll be judged for not being able to handle the situation on our own.

The truth is, we all need help from time to time. Asking for help is a sign of strength, not weakness.

When we're feeling overwhelmed, it's important to remember that we don't have to go through it alone. There are people in our lives who are willing to help us, and it's OK to ask for their support. Whether it's a friend, family member, or professional, it's important to reach out and ask for help.

When we ask for help, we're taking a step towards solving our problem. We're taking responsibility for our situation and taking action to make it better. And when we do, we're showing ourselves that we're strong enough to handle whatever comes our way.

So the next time you're feeling overwhelmed, remember that it really is OK to ask for help. It doesn't make you weak; it makes you strong.

We all know that life can be difficult at times, and that it's not always easy to ask for help when we need it. But it's important to remember that it's OK to be vulnerable and to reach out for support when we need it.

It can be hard to admit that we need help, especially when we're used to being independent and taking care of ourselves. But it's important to remember that asking for help is a sign of strength, not weakness.

It shows that we're willing to take responsibility for our own wellbeing and that we're open to accepting help from others.

When we're feeling overwhelmed or struggling to cope, it's OK to reach out for help. Whether it's talking to a friend, family member, or professional, it's important to remember that there are people who are willing to listen and offer support.

At the end of the day, it's OK to be vulnerable and to ask for help when we need it. It's a sign of strength and courage, and it's important to remember that there are people who are willing to listen and offer support.

So don't be afraid to reach out and ask for help when you need it.

23

12. "Focus on what you can control and let go of the things you can't."

In today's world, it can be easy to get overwhelmed by the things that are out of our control.

From the news to our day-to-day lives, it can be hard to stay focused on the things that we can actually control. That's why it's important to remember the power of focusing on what we can control and letting go of the things we can't.

When we focus on what we can control, we can take actionable steps to make positive changes in our lives. We can set goals and work towards achieving them, instead of worrying about the things that are out of our control. We can also take the time to appreciate the small victories and successes that come from our hard work.

On the other hand, when we focus on the things we can't control, we can become overwhelmed and discouraged. We can become stuck in a cycle of worrying and ruminating on the things that are out of our control, instead of taking actionable steps to make positive changes.

The key to success is to identify and recognize the things we can control and focus on them, while simply turning our focus away from anything that we can't.

We can't control the news, the stock market, or the weather, but we can control our attitude, our actions, and our reactions. We can choose to focus on the positive and take actionable steps to make positive changes in our lives.

When we focus on what we can control, we can take control of our lives and create the life we want. We can take the time to appreciate the small successes and victories that come from our hard work.

We can also take the time to reflect on our progress and celebrate our successes.

So, the next time you're feeling overwhelmed, remember to focus on those things that you can control and let go of the things you can't.

*13. "Your feelings are valid, and so are your parents'
feelings."*

There is great importance in accepting your feelings and those of your
parents are valid. We all have different experiences and perspectives,
and it's important to recognize and respect those differences.

When it comes to our feelings, it's important to remember that they are
valid, no matter what. It's also important to remember that our parents'
feelings are valid too.

When we validate our own feelings, we are acknowledging that our
emotions are real and that we have the right to feel the way we do. This
can be especially helpful when we're feeling overwhelmed or frustrated.

By accepting our feelings, we can take a step back and recognize that
our feelings are valid and that we don't have to be ashamed of them.

Likewise, our parents' feelings are valid too. Our parents have their own
experiences and perspectives, and it's important to respect and validate
those.

We may not always agree with our parents, but it's important to
remember that their feelings are just as valid as ours.

Validating our own feelings and those of our parents can help us to better understand each other and to create a more harmonious relationship. It can also help us to better understand our own emotions and to recognize that we all have different experiences and perspectives.

By validating our feelings and those of our parents, we can create a more understanding and compassionate environment.

14. "Your parents' divorce does not define you — you can still create your own happy story."

Divorce is a difficult experience for anyone to go through, especially for older children and teenagers. It can be hard to make sense of the situation and to understand why it is happening.

It can be even harder to come to terms with the fact that your parents are no longer together. It can be easy to feel like the divorce is defining you and that it is the only story that will be told about your family.

However, what is important is that your parents' divorce does not define you. You can still create your own happy story, even if your parents' story has ended.

It is important to focus on the positives and to remember that you are still loved and supported by both of your parents, even if they are no longer together.

It is also good to be aware that you are not alone in this experience. There are many other children and teens who have gone through similar experiences and who can relate to what you are going through.

It can be helpful to reach out to these people and to talk about your feelings and experiences.

The bottom line is that you are in control of your own story. You can choose to focus on the positive aspects of your life and to create a story that is full of hope and happiness. You can choose to look forward to the future and to create a story that is full of joy and success.

No matter what your parents' story is or what the circumstances of their separation are, you can still create your own happy story.

15. "No matter the circumstances, you are always worthy of love and respect."

We all have moments in our lives when we feel like we're not worthy of love and respect, especially when we're feeling really down in the dumps.

It could be because of a mistake we've made, a difficult situation we're facing, or simply because of our own insecurities. But no matter what the circumstances are, it's important to remember that you are always worthy of love and respect.

It's easy to forget this when we're feeling down, but it's important to remind ourselves that we are worthy of love and respect. We may not always feel like we deserve it, but it's important to remember that we do.

We all make mistakes, and that doesn't make us any less worthy of love and respect.

It's also important to know that we can't always control the circumstances we're in. We may be facing difficult situations that are out of our control, but that doesn't mean we're any less worthy of love and respect.

We may not be able to control our circumstances, but we can control how we respond to them.

It's also important to understand that we can't always control how other people treat us. We may be treated unfairly or with disrespect, but that doesn't mean we're any less worthy of love and respect.

While we can't always control how other people treat us, we can control how we respond to it.

Always remember that you are worthy of love and respect. You may not always feel like you deserve it, but it's important to remind yourself that you do.

16. "You are strong enough to get through your parents' divorce and to come out even stronger."

Divorce is never easy, especially when it involves your own parents. It can be a difficult and confusing time, and it can be hard to know how to cope with the changes that come with it.

But despite everything that is going on, the fact is that you are strong enough to get through this difficult period in your life, whether you know it or not.

The first step is to accept that your parents are going through a divorce. It can be hard to come to terms with the fact that your family is changing, but it is important to recognize that this is a part of life.

It is also important to remember that your parents still love you, even if they are no longer together.

The next step is to talk to someone about your feelings. It can be helpful to talk to a trusted adult, such as a teacher or a family friend.

You can also talk to a counsellor or therapist if you feel like you need more support. Talking to someone can help you to process your emotions and to find ways to cope with the changes that come with your parents' divorce.

It is also important to take care of yourself during this time. Make sure to get enough sleep, eat healthy meals, and take time for yourself. Exercise can also be a great way to reduce stress and to help you stay positive.

Understand that you are strong enough to get through your parents' divorce. It may take some time, but you can come out of this period of your life even stronger.

You may even find that you have grown and learned a lot from the experience.

17. "You don't have to have all the answers right now."

We live in a world where we are constantly bombarded with information and it can be overwhelming to try and process it all. It can be tempting to try and have all the answers right away, but this can lead to making rushed decisions or overlooking important details.

The truth is, it's OK to not have all the answers right away. Taking the time to really think through a situation and consider all the options can be beneficial in the long run.

It's important to take a step back and look at the big picture before making any decisions. This can help you make sure that you are making the best decision for yourself and your situation.

Remember that whenever you're stuck on a problem, asking for help is totally OK. You don't have to have all the answers right away and it's perfectly acceptable to reach out to people who may have more knowledge or experience in the area.

This can be a great way to gain insight and perspective on a situation.

A potent takeaway from this point is that it's OK to take your time. There is no need to rush into a decision if you don't feel comfortable.

Taking the time to really think through a situation and make sure you are making the right decision can be beneficial in the long run.

At the end of the day, remember that may not have all the answers you need. That comes from just being human.

Taking the time to really think through a situation and consider all the options can be beneficial in the long run. But if you need help, you can always ask for it to help you when making decisions.

18. "Your parents still care about you, even if they make mistakes."

It's easy to feel like your parents don't care about you when they make mistakes. It can be hard to understand why they do the things they do, and it can be even harder to forgive them for it. But it's important to remember that your parents still care about you, even if they make mistakes.

No parent is perfect, and it's natural for them to make mistakes. Remember that your parents are human too, and they're doing their best to raise you. They may not always get it right, but they're still trying their best.

Importantly, your parents are likely doing the best they can with the resources they have. They may not have the same resources that other parents have, and they may not be able to provide you with everything you need. But they're still doing their best to make sure you have what you need.

Your parents, regardless of their situation, are trying to teach you important lessons. Even if their methods may not always be perfect, they're still trying to teach you valuable lessons that will help you in the future.

Remember that whatever mistakes they may make, your parents love you and care for you. They may not always show it in the way you want them to, but they still care about you and want the best for you. All the while, they're trying to do their best and they love you.

19. "You can create a new normal that works for you."

When your parents divorce, it can feel like your entire world has been turned upside down. The good news is that you can create a new normal that works for you.

Here are some tips to help you adjust to your new life after your parents' divorce.

1. Acknowledge Your Feelings

It's normal to feel a range of emotions after your parents' divorce. You may feel sad, angry, confused, or even relieved. It's important to acknowledge your feelings and give yourself time to process them.

Don't be afraid to talk to someone about how you're feeling. Talking to a trusted friend, family member, or therapist can help you work through your emotions.

2. Create a Support System

Having a strong support system is essential after your parents' divorce. Surround yourself with people who understand what you're going through and can provide emotional support. This could include family members, friends, teachers, or even a therapist.

Friends can be a great source of support during a divorce. They can provide a listening ear and a shoulder to cry on. They can also help you to stay positive and remind you that you are not alone.

Family members can also be a great source of support. They can provide emotional and practical support, such as helping with childcare or offering a place to stay. They can also provide a sense of stability and security in a time of upheaval.

Professionals, such as counsellors or therapists, can also be part of your support system. They can provide guidance and help you to process your emotions. They can also help you to develop coping strategies and provide a safe space to talk about your feelings.

3. Establish New Routines

Creating new routines can help you adjust to your new life after your parents' divorce. Establishing a regular schedule for meals, schoolwork, and activities can help you feel more in control of your life.

Creating a routine doesn't have to be complicated. Start by making a list of activities that you enjoy and that make you feel good. This could include things like going for a walk, reading a book, or listening to music.

Then, decide how often you want to do each activity. For example, you could decide to go for a walk every day or read a book every other day.

Creating a routine can also help you stay organized. Once you have your list of activities, create a schedule that works for you.

You can use a calendar, planner, or even a simple list to keep track of your routine. Make sure to include time for yourself, as well as time to spend with family and friends.

4. Find Healthy Ways to Cope

It's important to find healthy ways to cope with your emotions. Exercise, journaling, eating a healthy diet and spending time with friends can all help you manage your stress.

Avoid unhealthy coping mechanisms, such as using drugs or alcohol, as these can make your situation a whole lot worse. Also, avoid falling into unhealthy habits like eating a lot of comfort foods such as cakes, cookies, pastries, doughnuts and candy bars as these will just cause you to gain weight, break out in spots and may even make you feel worse in the long run.

5. Focus on the Positive

It can be hard to focus on the positive when your parents are divorcing, but it's important to know that divorce is a difficult and emotional experience for everyone involved, especially for older children and teenagers.

When your parents are divorcing, it may seem hard to focus on the positive and it can be easy to get caught up in the negative emotions. Yet even though your parents are divorcing, they still love you and will continue to be a part of your life going forward.

Divorce doesn't necessarily have to be a negative experience. It can be an opportunity for your parents to find happiness and for you to find a new sense of balance in your life. It can also be a chance for you to learn how to be independent and to develop new relationships with both of your parents.

It's important to talk to your parents about their divorce and to express your feelings. It can also be helpful to talk to a trusted adult, such as a teacher, counsellor, or another family member about how you're feeling. Talking to someone can help you process your emotions and can help you find ways to cope with the changes in your life.

It can also be helpful to find activities that you enjoy and that help you relax. Exercise, art, music, and spending time with friends can all be great ways to take your mind off of the divorce and to focus on the positive.

Since there are many other children and teenagers who are going through the same experience as you, there are many resources available to help you. Reach out to your school, church, or community centre for support.

Divorce can be a difficult experience, but it doesn't have to be a negative one. Remember to focus on the positive and to reach out for help when you need it.

20. *"Your story matters and it's OK to share it."*

Your patents' divorce can be a confusing and overwhelming time, and it can be difficult to know how to cope with the changes that come with it. Everyone's experience of their parents' divorce can be different, and it is perfectly acceptable to share your experience with others.

No matter how you feel about your parents' divorce, the main thing to be aware of is that it is not your fault. It is not your responsibility to try to fix the situation or make it better.

It is also OK to feel whatever emotions come up during this time. You may feel sad, angry, scared, or confused. It is important to allow yourself to feel these emotions and to talk to someone about them.

Your parents' divorce does not define you. You are still the same person you were before the divorce, and you can still have a happy and fulfilling life. It is also important to remember that you can still have a relationship with both of your parents, even if they are no longer together.

There are also many resources available to help you cope with the changes that come with your parents' divorce.

You can still have a happy and fulfilling life after your parents have divorced and gone their separate ways. It may take some time to adjust to the changes, but with the right support and resources, you can find a way to move forward.

21. "You have the power to find joy and peace even in difficult times."

Finding joy and peace in difficult times can be a challenge, but it is possible. It requires us to look beyond our current circumstances and focus on the positive aspects of our lives.

We must also be mindful of our thoughts and feelings, and take steps to cultivate a sense of gratitude and appreciation for the good things in our lives.

One way to find joy and peace in difficult times is to practice mindfulness. This involves being aware of our thoughts and feelings in the present moment, without judgment or attachment.

Mindfulness can help us to stay grounded and focused on the present, rather than worrying about the future or ruminating on the past. It can also help us to be more aware of our emotions, so that we can better manage them and find ways to cope with difficult situations.

Another way to find joy and peace in difficult times is to practice gratitude. Gratitude involves taking the time to appreciate the good things in our lives, no matter how small. This could be something as simple as appreciating a beautiful sunset, or taking the time to thank someone for their kindness.

Practising gratitude can help us to focus on the positive aspects of our lives, and can help us to find joy and peace even in difficult times. We can take time to appreciate the people who have helped us, the things that we have, and the opportunities that we have been given.

Gratitude is a powerful emotion that can have a profound effect on our lives. It can help us to appreciate the good things in life and to focus on the positive aspects of our lives.

Practising gratitude can help us to cultivate a more positive outlook, to be more mindful of our blessings, and to be more grateful for the people and good things in our lives.

We can take time to appreciate the little things, such as a beautiful sunset or a kind gesture from a friend. We can also take time to appreciate the bigger things, such as a successful school term or getting better at sports. By taking the time to appreciate the good things in our lives, we can become more mindful of our blessings and be more grateful for them.

The important fact here is that we need to take care of ourselves during difficult times. This could involve engaging in activities that bring us joy, such as reading a book, listening to music, or going for a walk.

It could also involve reaching out to friends and family for support, or seeking professional help if needed. Taking care of ourselves can help us

to find joy and peace in difficult times, and can help us to stay resilient
and cope with whatever life throws our way.

22. "You are worthy of being loved and having a happy life."

We all deserve to be loved and to have a happy life. Unfortunately, life can be difficult and it can be hard to remember that we are worthy of love and happiness.

That's why it's important to take the time to remind ourselves that we are worthy of love and a happy life.

When we take the time to remind ourselves that we are worthy of love and a happy life, we can start to make positive changes in our lives. We can start to focus on the things that make us happy and that bring us joy.

We can start to make time for the people and activities that bring us joy. We can start to take better care of ourselves, both physically and mentally. We can start to make healthier choices and create healthier habits.

We can also start to focus on the things that we are grateful for. When we take the time to appreciate the good things in our lives, it can help us to feel more positive and to be more mindful of the things that we have.

It can also help us to be more mindful of the things that we want to change in our lives.

When we take the time to remind ourselves that we are worthy of love and a happy life, we can start to make positive changes in our lives. We can start to focus on the things that make us happy and that bring us joy.

We can start to make time for the people and activities that bring us joy. We can start to take better care of ourselves, both physically and mentally. We can start to make healthier choices and create healthier habits.

Most importantly, we can start to love ourselves and to be kind to ourselves. We can start to recognize our own worth and to treat ourselves with respect.

We can start to forgive ourselves for our mistakes and to be more compassionate with ourselves.

23. "It's OK to take time for yourself and to focus on your own needs."

Taking time for yourself is an important part of self-care. It can be hard to make time for yourself when you're busy with work, family, and other commitments, but it's essential for your mental and physical health.

Taking time for yourself can help you relax, recharge, and refocus.

When you take time for yourself, it's important to focus on your own needs. This could mean taking a break from work to go for a walk, reading a book, or just taking a few moments to sit and relax.

Remember to make sure you're getting enough sleep, eating healthy, and exercising regularly.

Taking time for yourself can also mean doing activities that make you happy. This could be anything from going to the movies, playing sports, to spending time with friends.

It's important to make sure you're doing things that make you feel good and that bring you joy.

It's worth knowing that taking time for yourself doesn't have to be expensive or time-consuming. Even small things like taking a few minutes to meditate or writing in a journal can make a big difference in your mental and physical health.

Taking time for yourself is an important part of self-care. It can help you relax, recharge, and refocus. It can also help you do things that make you happy and that bring you joy.

So make sure you take the time to focus on your own needs and do things that make you feel good.

24. "Don't be a slave to your fears. Be the master of your destiny."

Are you a slave to your fears? Do you let them dictate your life and your decisions? If so, it's time to take control and become the master of your destiny.

Fear can be a powerful emotion, and it can be hard to break free from its grip. But it's important to remember that you are in control of your life and your decisions. You don't have to let fear dictate your choices.

The first step to becoming the master of your destiny is to recognize your fears. What are you afraid of?

- Are you afraid of failure?
- Are you afraid of success?
- Are you afraid of taking risks?
- Are you afraid of what other people might think of you?

Once you've identified your fears, you can start to take steps to overcome them.

One way to do this is to challenge your fears. Ask yourself why you're afraid and if there's any evidence that your fear is justified.

Often, we fear things that are unlikely to happen or that we can't control. Once you've identified the source of your fear, you can start to take steps to address it.

Another way to become the master of your destiny is to focus on what you can control. Instead of worrying about things that are out of your control, focus on the things that you can influence.

This could be your attitude, your actions, or your environment. By taking control of these things, you can start to take control of your life.

Finally, take action. Don't let fear stop you from taking risks and making changes. Take small steps and be patient with yourself. It's OK to make mistakes and to learn from them.

Instead of allowing fear to dictate your choices, face them down and take control of any situation. Take action and start living the life you want. By taking control of your life and your decisions, you can be in charge of your destiny.

25. "You can find a way to make sense of the chaos that divorce creates."

Divorce can be a difficult and chaotic time for everyone involved. It can be hard to make sense of the emotions and changes that come with it.

But there are ways to cope and make sense of the chaos that divorce creates.

First, it's important to remember that you are not alone. Divorce is a common experience, and there are many people who have gone through it and come out the other side. Reach out to family, friends, and professionals for support.

Second, take time to process your emotions. Divorce can bring up a range of emotions, from sadness to anger to relief.

Allow yourself to feel whatever comes up, and don't be afraid to talk about it.

Third, focus on self-care. Take time to do things that make you feel good, such as exercising, reading, or spending time with friends. Make sure to get enough sleep, eat healthy, and take breaks when needed.

Fourth, make a plan for the future. It can be helpful to make a list of goals and steps to take to achieve them. This can help you focus on the positive and create a sense of purpose.

Finally, remember that divorce is a process. It can take time to adjust to the changes, and it's important to be patient with yourself.

Take things one day at a time, and don't be afraid to ask for help when needed.

26. "No matter how hard it is, you are never alone."

Divorce is one of the most difficult experiences a person can go through. It can be emotionally draining, financially challenging, and can leave you feeling isolated and alone.

But it's important to remember that you are never alone while on your journey. There are many resources available to help you through this difficult time.

First and foremost, it's important to take care of yourself. Make sure you're getting enough rest, eating healthy, and taking time for yourself to relax and unwind. Exercise can be a great way to reduce stress and help you stay in shape.

It's also important to talk to someone about your feelings. Whether it's a friend, family member, or therapist, having someone to talk to can help you process your emotions and work through the challenges of divorce.

There are also many support groups available for those going through divorce. These groups can provide a safe space to talk about your experiences and connect with others who are going through similar situations.

Many of these groups are free or low-cost, and can be found online or through local organizations.

Want to know something else really helpful? Fact: There are many other teenagers who have gone through their parents' divorce and come out the other side.

You can find strength and comfort in knowing that you are not alone in your struggles. With the right support and resources, you can make it through this difficult time and come out stronger on the other side.

27. "You can choose to find a new way to live and be happy."

Divorce can be especially hard and emotionally draining for teenagers who are caught in the middle of their parents' separation.

As a teen, it can be difficult to understand why your parents are divorcing and how it will affect your life. It can be a confusing and overwhelming time, but it is important to remember that you can find a way to be happy and live a fulfilling life even after your parents' divorce.

The first step to finding a new way to live and be happy after the separation is to accept the situation. It can be difficult to accept that your parents are no longer together, but it is important to understand that it is not your fault and that it is something that you cannot control.

Once you have accepted the situation, it is important to talk to your parents and other trusted adults about how you are feeling. Talking to someone can help you to process your emotions and understand the situation better.

Another way to find a new way to live and be happy is to focus on the positive aspects of your life. It can be easy to get caught up in the negative emotions associated with the divorce, but it is important to remember that there are still many positive things in your life.

Spend time with friends and family, pursue hobbies and interests, and focus on the things that make you happy.

It is a well known fact that there are many others going through a similar experience to you. There are plenty of resources available to help you cope with the emotions associated with your parents' divorce.

Reach out to family, friends, and professionals for support and guidance. You can also join support groups and talk to other people who have gone through similar experiences.

28. "It's OK to feel scared, but don't forget that you are brave."

It's normal to feel scared in certain situations, especially when we are faced with something that is unfamiliar or uncertain.

Fear can be a powerful emotion that can make us feel overwhelmed and helpless. But it's important to remember that even in the face of fear, we can still be brave. Bravery doesn't mean that we don't feel scared.

It means that despite our fear, we are still willing to take action and face our fears. It means that we are willing to take risks and push ourselves out of our comfort zone. It means that we are willing to take a chance and try something new, even if it scares us.

When we are brave, we are able to take control of our lives and make positive changes. We can take steps to overcome our fears and become more confident in ourselves.

We can learn to trust our instincts and make decisions that are best for us. We can also learn to be more resilient and bounce back from difficult situations.

Being brave doesn't mean that we have to be fearless. It means that we are willing to face our fears, even when we are scared. It means that we are willing to be brave and make the best of every situation.

61

29. *"Your experiences will make you a stronger person."*

It can be difficult to understand why your parents are no longer together and why your family is changing.

It can be hard to accept that things will never be the same again. But whether you believe it or not, your experiences will give you strength in the face of adversity.

Divorce can be a difficult time for a teenager, but it is important to remember that it is no fault of your own. Your parents still love you and that they are doing what is best for the family.

There are many other teenagers who have gone through similar experiences and you can find support and understanding from them. You can still have a happy and healthy life after your parents' divorce. You can still have a strong relationship with both of your parents and you can still have a successful future.

Divorce can be a difficult experience, but it can also be an opportunity for growth. It can be a chance to learn how to be more independent and how to take care of yourself. It can also be a chance to discover a better understanding of live and become more compassionate towards others.

Your experiences with divorce can teach you how to cope with difficult situations and how to be resilient in the face of adversity. You will also learn how to be more independent and how to take care of yourself.

63

30. "It's OK to feel hurt, but remember that you are strong."

We all experience hurt in our lives, whether it's from a broken relationship, a difficult situation, or a traumatic event. It's important to acknowledge and accept these feelings, rather than trying to ignore them or push them away.

When we feel hurt, it's natural to want to protect ourselves from further pain. We may try to avoid the situation or person that caused us pain, or we may try to numb our feelings with drugs or alcohol.

The problem is that these strategies don't actually help us heal. In fact, they can make the pain worse in the long run.

Instead, it's important to recognize and accept our feelings of hurt. This doesn't mean that we have to stay in a state of pain forever. It simply means that we acknowledge our feelings and give ourselves permission to feel them. This can be a difficult process, but it's an important step in the healing process.

We may feel weak or vulnerable in the moment, but we have the strength to get through this. We can find comfort in the knowledge that we have the power to heal and move forward.

No matter how much pain we feel, we can find strength in ourselves. We can take comfort in the knowledge that we are capable of healing and moving forward. So, if you're feeling hurt, remember that you are strong.

65

31. "You have the strength to work through your feelings and find a way to be happy."

We all experience moments of sadness, anger, and frustration when our parents separate. It can seem hard to find the strength to push through it.

But it is possible to find a way to be happy. And it starts with understanding our emotions and how they affect us.

The first step is to recognize your feelings and accept them. It's important to acknowledge your emotions and give yourself permission to feel them. This can be difficult, but it's important to remember that your feelings are valid and that it's OK to feel them.

The next step is to identify the source of your emotions. You can do this by asking yourself questions such as:

- "What is causing me to feel this way?"
- "What is triggering this emotion?"

Once you have identified the source, you can start to work through it.

You can also try to find ways to cope with your emotions. This could include talking to a friend, writing in a journal, or engaging in a calming sports activity such as cycling or swimming. It's important to find a coping mechanism that works for you and to practice it regularly.

Focus on the positive. Remind yourself of the things that make you happy and focus on the good in your life. You can and should also practice gratitude and appreciation for the things you have.

Finding a way to be happy is possible, but it takes time and effort. It's important to be patient with yourself and to remember that it's OK to feel your emotions.

With the right tools and support, you can work through your feelings and find a way to be happy.

32. "It's OK to be honest with yourself and your feelings."

We often try to push away our emotions and ignore them, thinking that it will make us feel better. But the truth is, being honest with yourself and your feelings is an important part of self-care and emotional wellbeing.

When we are honest with ourselves, we can better understand our emotions and why we are feeling the way we do. This can help us to process our feelings and take steps to address them.

It can also help us to recognize patterns in our behaviour and make changes to improve our mental health.

Being honest with ourselves also means being honest about our needs and wants. We need to be able to recognize when we are feeling overwhelmed or stressed, and take steps to address those feelings.

We also need to be honest about our desires and goals, and take steps to make them a reality.

Finally, being honest with ourselves means being honest about our mistakes and failures. We need to be able to recognize when we have made a mistake or failed at something, and take steps to learn from it and move forward.

Being honest with yourself and your feelings is an important part of self-care and emotional wellbeing. It can help you to better understand your emotions, recognize patterns in your behaviour, and take steps to address your needs and wants.

It can also help to learn from your mistakes and failures, and move forward. So, it's completely OK to be honest with yourself and your feelings.

33. "Your story is unique, powerful and life-changing and its message can help others in a similar situation."

We all have stories that shape our lives and define who we are. Being a teenager going through their parents' divorce is one of these experiences that can seem overwhelming to you.

Are you struggling with a difficult life experience? Are you feeling overwhelmed and unsure of how to move forward?

Many people have faced similar challenges and have found ways to cope and grow from them.

Divorce is a difficult and life-changing experience for anyone, but it can be especially difficult for teenagers. As a teenager, you may feel like your world is being turned upside down, and it can be hard to know how to cope with the changes.

Here are some tips for navigating the experience of your parents' divorce as a teenager:

First, it's important to remember that you are not alone. Many teenagers go through the experience of their parents' divorce, and it's important to reach out to friends and family for support. Talking to someone who has gone through a similar experience can be especially helpful.

Second, it's important to take care of yourself. This may mean taking time to do things that make you feel good, such as spending time with friends, exercising, or engaging in activities that you enjoy. It's also important to make sure you are eating healthy and getting enough sleep.

Third, it's important to stay connected with both of your parents. Even if you don't agree with their decisions, it's important to maintain a relationship with both of them. This can be difficult, but it's important to know that your parents still love you and want what's best for you.

Finally, be patient with yourself. Divorce is a difficult process, and it can take time to adjust to the changes.

It's important to be kind to yourself and to give yourself time to process your emotions, and you can navigate this experience with strength and resilience.

34. "It's OK to take a break and give yourself some time to heal."

Taking a break and giving yourself time to heal from the stresses of parents divorcing is an important part of self-care.

It can be hard to take a break when you're feeling overwhelmed or exhausted, but it is essential for your mental and physical health. Taking a break can help you to recharge, refocus, and reconnect with yourself.

When you're feeling overwhelmed, it can be helpful to take a step back and give yourself some time to process your emotions. This could mean taking a few days off work, or even just taking a few hours to yourself.

Remember that taking a break doesn't mean you're giving up or giving in. It's a way to give yourself the space and time you need to heal and move forward.

When you're taking a break, it's important to focus on activities that help you to relax and recharge. This could include taking a walk, reading a book, listening to music, or spending time with friends and family.

It's also important to practice self-care activities such as getting enough sleep, eating healthy, and exercising.

Taking a break can also be a great opportunity to reflect on your life and your goals. It's a chance to think about what's important to you and to make plans for the future.

It's also a chance to practice self-compassion and to forgive yourself for any mistakes or missteps you've made.

Taking a break doesn't mean you're giving up. It's a way to give yourself the time and space you need to heal and move forward.

So don't be afraid to take a break and give yourself the time you need to heal.

35. "Take one step at a time and you will get through this."

Are you feeling overwhelmed? It's a feeling that many of us experience at some point in our lives.

Whether it's due to a heavy workload, a difficult situation, or a combination of both, feeling overwhelmed can be incredibly stressful and can leave us feeling helpless and stuck.

But it doesn't have to be that way. There are steps you can take to help you manage your feelings of overwhelm and get back on track. Here are some tips to help you get started:

1. Acknowledge your feelings. It's important to recognize and accept your feelings of overwhelm. Acknowledging your feelings can help you to better understand why you're feeling overwhelmed and can help you to take steps to address the issue.

2. Break down the problem. When you're feeling overwhelmed, it can be helpful to break down the problem into smaller, more manageable pieces. This can help you to better understand the issue and can make it easier to tackle.

3. Prioritize. Once you've broken down the problem, it's important to prioritize the tasks that need to be done. This will help you to focus on the most important tasks first and can help you to stay on track.

4. Take breaks. Taking breaks throughout the day can help to reduce stress and can help you to stay focused. Taking a few minutes to step away from the problem can help you to clear your head and can help you to come back to the task with a fresh perspective.

5. Ask for help. Don't be afraid to ask for help when you're feeling overwhelmed. Whether it's a friend, family member, or colleague, asking for help can help to lighten the load and can help you to get back on track.

Remember, feeling overwhelmed is a normal part of life. But with the right strategies, you can get through the experience and come out of it a stronger person.

36. "You can choose to channel your energy into something positive."

We all have days when we feel like we're stuck in a rut and can't seem to find the motivation to do anything productive. It can be hard to break out of this cycle, but it is possible. One way to do this is to channel your energy into something positive.

When you're feeling down, it can be easy to get caught up in negative thoughts and feelings. This can lead to a lack of motivation and a feeling of being stuck. To break out of this cycle, it's important to focus on something positive.

One way to do this is to focus on something that you're passionate about. Whether it's a hobby, a project, or something else, it's important to find something that you're passionate about and focus on it. This can help to give you a sense of purpose and direction, and can help to motivate you to take action.

Another way to channel your energy into something positive is to focus on self-care. Taking time for yourself to relax and recharge can help to give you the energy and motivation to tackle whatever tasks you have ahead of you. This could be anything from taking a walk, reading a book, or even just taking a few minutes to meditate.

By putting your energy into something positive, you can break out of the cycle of feeling stuck and unmotivated. Whether it's focusing on something that you're passionate about, taking time for self-care, or simply taking a break from everything, these are all great ways to help you get back on track.

37. "Don't put up with being lied to. Demand and expect the truth always."

Divorce can be a difficult and emotional time for everyone involved, especially older children and teenagers.

When parents divorce, it can be hard to know how to handle the situation. It's important to remember that you have the right to demand and expect the truth from your parents.

Lying to children during a divorce can be damaging and can make the situation even more difficult. It can be hard to tell when someone is lying, but it's important to be aware of the signs.

If your parents are not being honest with you, it's important to speak up and let them know that you expect the truth.

It's also important to always remember that you are not responsible for your parents' divorce. It's not your fault and you should never feel like you have to take sides. Always know that your parents still love you and that they are going through a difficult time.

It's good to know that you can get support from people close to you. There are many resources available to help you cope with the emotions and stress of your parents' divorce.

Talking to a trusted adult, such as a teacher, counsellor, or family friend, can be a great way to get the support you need.

79

It's worth remembering that you can still have a healthy relationship with both of your parents. Even though they are no longer together, they both still love you and want what's best for you.

However, at the end of the day, that relationship you have with both of your parents, even if they are divorced, will be stronger when they are completely honest with you, and you with them.

38. "You are resilient and capable of handling anything that comes your way."

Resilience is an important trait to have in life. It is the ability to bounce back from difficult situations and to keep going despite the challenges that come our way.

It is a trait that can be developed and strengthened over time.

When faced with difficult situations, it is important to remember that we are resilient and capable of handling anything that comes our way. We can use our resilience to help us cope with difficult times and to stay focused on our goals.

One way to build resilience is to practice self-care. Taking time for yourself to relax and recharge can help you stay focused and motivated. It is also important to practice positive self-talk and to remind yourself of your strengths and capabilities.

Another way to build resilience is to reach out for help when needed. It is important to remember that there are people who can help you. Talking to a friend, family member, or professional can be a great way to get the support you need.

Resilience is not something that happens overnight. It takes time and effort to build resilience, but it is worth it in the end. With practice and dedication, you can become more resilient and better equipped to handle life's challenges.

39. "You have the power to create a life that you love."

Creating a life that you love is a powerful thing. It's something that can bring you joy, fulfilment, and a sense of purpose. But it's not always easy. It takes time, effort, and dedication to create a life that you truly love.

The first step in creating a life that you love is to identify what it is that you want. You can start be asking yourself the following questions:

- What do you want your life to look like?
- What kind of career do you want?
- What kind of relationships do you want?
- What kind of lifestyle do you want?

Once you have a clear vision of what you want, you can start taking steps to make it happen.

The next step is to create a plan. You can outline your plan by asking yourself questions like:

- What steps do you need to take to get to where you want to be?
- What resources do you need?
- What kind of support do you need?

Having a plan will help you stay focused and motivated.

Once you have a plan, it's time to take action. This is where the hard work comes in. You have to be willing to put in the time and effort to make your dreams a reality. It may not necessarily be easy, but it will be worth it.

Finally, don't forget to take care of yourself. Make sure you're getting enough rest, eating healthy, and taking time to relax and enjoy life. Taking care of yourself is essential to creating a life that you love.

Creating a life that you love is a process. It takes time, effort, and dedication. But it's worth it.

When you create a life that you love, you'll be happier, more fulfilled, and more motivated to keep going. So never give up. Keep going and you'll get there.

40. "No matter how hard it gets, you will make it through."

Are you feeling overwhelmed and struggling to make it through life's challenges?

You're not alone. Life can be difficult and it's easy to feel like you're not going to make it through. But no matter how hard it gets, you can stay strong and make it through. You've got this!

It might not seem like it, butt you are strong and capable of overcoming any obstacle. You have the power to make it through any situation, no matter how difficult it may seem.

Here are some tips to help you stay strong and make it through life's challenges:

1. Take a break. When things get tough, it's important to take a step back and give yourself a break. Take some time to relax and recharge. This will help you clear your mind and gain perspective on the situation.

2. Reach out for help. Don't be afraid to ask for help when you need it. Talk to a friend, family member, or professional for support. They can provide a listening ear and offer advice to help you get through the tough times.

3. Focus on the positives. It's easy to get caught up in the negatives, but try to focus on the positives in your life. Remind yourself of all the good things you have going for you and the progress you've made.

4. Take care of yourself. Make sure you're taking care of your physical and mental health. Get enough sleep, eat healthy, exercise, and do things that make you feel good.

5. Believe in yourself. Believe that you can make it through any situation. Remind yourself of your strength and resilience and that you can handle anything that comes your way.

No matter how hard things get in life, you can make it through.

41. "Pain may be inevitable, but suffering is always optional"

Pain is an unavoidable part of life. We all experience physical and emotional pain at some point in our lives, and it can be difficult to cope with.

However, while pain may be inevitable, suffering is not. Suffering is the emotional and mental anguish that can come with pain, and it is something that we can choose to avoid.

The key to avoiding suffering is to recognize that pain is a natural part of life and to accept it as such. When we can accept pain as a part of life, we can learn to cope with it in a healthy way. This means learning to recognize our own emotional and mental triggers and developing strategies to manage them.

One way to do this is to practice mindfulness. Mindfulness is the practice of being present in the moment and accepting whatever is happening without judgment. It can help us to recognize our own emotional and mental triggers and to develop strategies to manage them.

Another way to avoid suffering is to practice self-care. Self-care is the practice of taking care of ourselves physically, emotionally, and mentally.

This can include things like getting enough sleep, eating healthy, exercising, and engaging in activities that bring us joy. By taking care of ourselves, we can better manage our pain and reduce our suffering.

It is important to know that we are not alone in our pain. We can reach out to friends, family, and professionals for support and guidance.

Having a strong support system can help us to cope with our pain and reduce our suffering.

Pain may be inevitable, but suffering is always optional. By practising mindfulness, self-care, and reaching out for support, we can learn to cope with our pain in a healthy way and avoid unnecessary suffering.

42. "There are many resources available to help you cope with the changes."

It can be hard to adjust to the changes that come with your parents' divorce, but there are many resources available to help you cope. It's important to take care of yourself, talk to someone, find a support system, and seek professional help if needed.

Here are some tips to help you navigate through this difficult time:

1. Talk to someone: It's important to talk to someone about your feelings and experiences. This could be a family member, friend, teacher, or counsellor. Talking to someone can help you process your emotions and provide you with support.

2. Take care of yourself: Make sure to take care of yourself during this time. Get plenty of rest, eat healthy, and exercise. Taking care of yourself will help you stay strong and cope with the changes.

3. Find a support system: Find a support system of people who can help you through this difficult time. This could be family, friends, or even a support group. Having a support system can help you feel less alone and provide you with emotional support.

4. Find activities you enjoy: Find activities that you enjoy and make you feel good. This could be sports, art, music, or anything else that you find enjoyable. Doing activities that make you happy can help you cope with the changes.

5. Seek professional help: If you are having difficulty coping with the changes, it may be helpful to seek professional help. A therapist or counsellor can provide you with additional support and help you work through your emotions.

Even though a divorce can be a difficult and emotional time, there are lots of resources that can help you cope with the situation. With the right support, you can get through this difficult time.

43. "Your perspective on life has the power to shape your reality."

Life is full of ups and downs, and it can be difficult to stay positive when faced with adversity.

Yet did you know that our perspective on life has the power to shape our reality? When we take a positive outlook on life, we can find the strength to overcome any obstacle that comes our way.

Having a positive perspective on life means looking for the good in any situation, no matter how bad it may look at first glance.

It means finding the silver lining in the clouds, and recognizing that every experience, good or bad, can be a learning opportunity. It means being grateful for the blessings we have, and recognizing that even in difficult times, there is something to be thankful for.

It also means having a growth mindset. Instead of seeing failure as a sign of weakness, we can use it as an opportunity to learn and grow. We can recognize that mistakes are part of the process, and that they can help us become better versions of ourselves.

It also means being kind to ourselves and others. We can practice self-compassion and recognize that we are all doing the best we can. We can also be kind to others, and recognize that everyone is fighting their own battles.

Finally, having a positive perspective on life means having faith, both in ourselves and in our ability to overcome adversity.

We can have faith that things will work out in the end, and that we will be able to overcome any challenge that comes our way. We can have faith that we are capable of achieving our goals, and that we are worthy of love and happiness.

Having a positive perspective on life can be difficult, but it is worth the effort. When we take a positive outlook on life, we can find the strength to overcome any obstacle that comes our way.

We can find the courage to take risks, and the resilience to keep going even when things get tough. We can find the joy in life, and the hope that tomorrow will be better than today.

44. "You can find joy in the little things and make them into something special."

We all have days when it feels like nothing is going right and it's hard to find joy in anything.

Yet despite what might be going on around us, real joy can be found in the little things. It's easy to get caught up in the hustle and bustle of life and forget to take a moment to appreciate the small moments that bring us joy.

One way to find joy in the little things is to take time to appreciate the beauty of nature. Whether it's a walk in the park, a hike in the woods, or just sitting in your backyard, taking time to appreciate the beauty of nature can bring a sense of peace and joy.

Another way to find joy in the little things is to take time to appreciate the people in your life. Whether it's a friend, family member, or even a stranger, taking time to appreciate the people in your life can bring a sense of joy and connection.

Finally, taking time to appreciate the simple pleasures in life can bring a sense of joy. Whether it's a hot cup of coffee, a warm bath, or a good book, taking time to appreciate the simple pleasures in life can bring a sense of joy and contentment.

Finding joy in the little things can seem like a challenge at first, but with your growing awareness you'll find that joy can be found in the small moments.

93

Taking time to appreciate the beauty of nature, the people in your life, and the simple pleasures in life can bring a sense of joy and contentment.

So take a moment to appreciate the little things and make them into something special.

45. "Your future is still unwritten and you have the power to make it your own."

We all have the ability to shape our lives and create the future we want for ourselves. It's up to us to take the initiative and make the most of our lives.

The first step in creating your own future is to set goals. Think about what you want to achieve in life and make a plan to get there. Set realistic goals that you can work towards and make sure to break them down into smaller, achievable steps.

Once you have your goals in place, it's time to take action. Take the necessary steps to reach your goals and don't be afraid to take risks. You may not always succeed, but it's important to keep trying and never give up.

It's also important to stay positive and believe in yourself. Believe that you can achieve your goals and that you are capable of making your dreams come true. Surround yourself with positive people and stay motivated.

Despite the many trials of life's ups and downs, don't forget to enjoy the journey. Life is full of surprises and you never know what's around the corner. Embrace the unknown and enjoy the process of creating your own future.

Creating your own future is an empowering experience. It's up to you to take control of your life and make the most of it. So, take the initiative and make your future your own.

46. "It's OK to make mistakes in life and learn from them."

Making mistakes is an inevitable part of life. We all make mistakes, and it's important to remember that it's OK to make them as long as they teach us something useful.

But did you know that mistakes can also be a great learning opportunity, and can help us grow and become better versions of ourselves?

When we make mistakes, it's important to take responsibility for them. Acknowledge the mistake, apologize if necessary, and take steps to make sure it doesn't happen again.

It's also important to forgive yourself for making the mistake. We are all human and make mistakes, and it's important to remember that.

It's also important to learn from our mistakes. Ask yourself what you can do differently next time, and how you can prevent the same mistake from happening again. Reflect on the situation and think about what you can do differently in the future.

Making mistakes is a part of life. When we truly learn a lesson from our mistakes, we are far less likely to ever make the same ones again! Take responsibility for the mistakes you make, forgive yourself for making them, and learn something useful from them.

97

47. "You can be strong and resilient in the face of adversity."

We all face adversity in our lives, whether it be a difficult situation or a challenging obstacle.

It can seem hard to stay strong and resilient when faced with an adverse situation, but it is possible. Here are some tips to help you stay strong and resilient in the face of adversity:

1. Acknowledge Your Feelings: It's important to acknowledge and accept your feelings, whatever they may be. Acknowledging your feelings can help you to process them and move forward.

2. Take Care of Yourself: Taking care of your physical and mental health is essential when facing adversity. Make sure to get enough sleep, eat healthy, and take time to relax.

3. Reach Out for Support: Don't be afraid to reach out to friends and family for support. Talking to someone can help you to process your feelings and gain perspective.

4. Focus on What You Can Control: It's important to focus on the things that you can control, rather than worrying about things that are out of your control.

5. Practice Self-Compassion: It's important to be kind to yourself and practice self-compassion. Remind yourself that everyone faces adversity and that it's OK to make mistakes.

By following these tips, you can stay strong and resilient in the face of adversity.

Remember that adversity is a part of life, and it's OK to feel overwhelmed at times. With a little bit of self-care and support, you can get through it.

48. "Let your actions speak louder than your words."

We've all heard the phrase "actions speak louder than words", but what does it really mean?

In essence, it's a reminder that our actions have a greater impact than our words. We can say one thing, but if our actions don't match up, then our words will be meaningless.

This phrase is especially relevant in today's world, where we're constantly bombarded with messages from all angles. It's easy to get caught up in the noise and forget that our actions are more powerful than our words.

When it comes to making an impact, it's important to remember that our actions speak louder than our words. We can talk a good game, but if we don't back it up with action, then our words will be empty.

For example, if we say we're going to do something, but then don't follow through, then our words will be meaningless. On the other hand, if we take action and follow through on our promises, then our words will carry more weight.

It's also important to remember that our actions can have a lasting impact. We can say something in the moment, but if our actions don't match up, then our words will be forgotten.

On the other hand, if we take action and follow through on our promises, then our words will have a lasting impact.

Never forget that our actions can have a ripple effect. We can do something small, but if it has a positive impact, then it can have a lasting effect.

Remember that anyone can talk a good game, but if it's not backed up with action, then those words will be meaningless. On the other hand, to walk the walk is way more credible than to merely talk the talk.

49. "You are capable of achieving your goals and creating a life you love."

Creating a life you love is something that we all strive for. It's a journey that requires dedication, hard work, and a positive attitude.

But it's also a journey that can be incredibly rewarding. A life you love is one that is filled with joy, passion, and purpose.

The first step in creating a life you love is to set goals. Goals give you something to work towards and help you stay focused.

When setting goals, make sure they are realistic and achievable. It's also important to break them down into smaller, more manageable tasks. This will help you stay on track and make progress towards your goals.

Once you have your goals in place, it's time to take action. This means taking the necessary steps to make your goals a reality.

This could include researching, networking, and taking classes. It could also mean making changes to your lifestyle, such as eating healthier or exercising more.

Taking action is the only way to make progress and move closer to achieving your goals.

Always remember that it's important to stay positive and believe in yourself. It's easy to get discouraged when things don't go as planned, but it's important to stay focused and keep going.

Remind yourself of why you set the goals in the first place and why achieving them is important to you.

Creating a life you love is a journey that requires dedication and hard work, but it's also a journey that can be incredibly rewarding. With the right attitude and a commitment to taking action, you can achieve your goals and create a life you love.

50. "You are enough, just as you are."

We all have days when we feel like we're not enough. We feel like we're not doing enough, we're not achieving enough, and we're not living up to our own expectations.

It's easy to get caught up in the comparison game and feel like we're not measuring up. But it's important to remember that we are enough, just as we are.

It's easy to get caught up in the idea that we need to be doing more, achieving more, and being more in order to be enough. But the truth is, we don't need to do any of those things in order to be enough.

We are enough, just as we are.

When we start to feel like we're not enough, it's important to take a step back and remind ourselves that we are enough. We don't need to do more, be more, or achieve more in order to be enough.

We are enough, just as we are.

It's also important to remember that our worth and value are not determined by what we do or achieve. Our worth and value come from within, and no amount of doing or achieving can change that.

We are enough, just as we are.

It's easy to get caught up in the idea that we need to be doing more, achieving more, and being more in order to be enough. But the truth is, we don't need to do any of those things in order to be enough.

We are enough, just as we are.

So the next time you start to feel like you're not enough, take a step back and remind yourself that you are enough, just as you are. You don't need to do more, be more, or achieve more in order to be enough.

Putting it All Together

Throughout this book, we have shared a grand total of fifty thought-provoking sayings, expressions and ideas that can help you to get through your parents' divorce and come out the other side feeling empowered, supported and enlightened.

This is an experience that a surprisingly large number of teenagers are stuck with, through absolutely no fault of their own and that they did nothing at all to cause. Yet actually knowing that you are not to blame for this in any way, shape or form can be a first step to managing the situation much better than you might expect.

So take heart from the messages and their expanded explanations in this book. Use whichever of them that resonate best with your individual feelings and feel the empowerment flowing through you when you discover that you are not alone and you are not powerless!

You may be wondering if, as author of this book, I'm a little closer to this subject than I've mentioned, until now.

Well, I can share that I, too, experienced my own parents' divorce when I was a teenager. It was a long time ago and back then, there was not the support available that there is now.

But time is a great healer and I can tell you from my own horrible experience that things do get better. I did manage to get through all the emotional crap that I and my siblings had to endure during that difficult and upsetting episode in my life and it did make me stronger as I grew to adulthood.

I didn't want it to happen. I didn't like going through it when it did happen. To be honest, it was a living nightmare while it was happening.

But it happened. I got through it. I survived!

Believe me when I tell you that you can too!